Romantic
Wedding Flowers

The Complete Guide to
Selecting Beautiful Flowers
for Your Wedding

Inquiries should be addressed to :
The John Henry Company
P.O. Box 17099
5800 W. Grand River Avenue
Lansing, MI 48901

Library of Congress
Catalog Card Number: 95-076758
ISBN 0-9630431-2-9

Published, printed and distributed by
The John Henry Company
Lansing, MI

Table of Contents

Planning Your Wedding Flowers — 7-16

Your Wedding Style 8
Ordering Your Wedding Flowers 9
Enhancing Your Wedding with Color 10
Popular Wedding Colors 11
Popular Wedding Flowers 12-13
Flower Availability 14-16

Flowers For Your Wedding — 17-66

Selecting Your Bridal Bouquet 18
Carrying Your Bouquet 18
Bouquet Styles and Flowers to Wear 19-44
Ceremony Flowers 45-56
Reception Flowers 57-66

Wedding Planning Information — 67-79

Wedding Plan at a Glance 68
Wedding Flower Checklist 69-70
Wedding Budget and Expenses 71
And the Planning Begins 72-73
Monthly Planning 74-79

Index — 80

MONTHLY FLOWER
Availability

January

Acacia	Genista	Leptospermum	Scabiosa
Amaryllis	Ginger	Lilac	Tulip
Anemone	Heather	Lily of the Valley	Viburnum
Bird of Paradise	Heliconia	Monkshood	Waxflower
Daffodil	Hyacinth	Narcissus	

February

Acacia	Ginger	Lily of the Valley	Scabiosa
Amaryllis	Heather	Lysimachia	Tuberose
Anemone	Heliconia	Monkshood	Tulip
Bird of Paradise	Hyacinth	Narcissus	Viburnum
Daffodil	Leptospermum	Ranunculus	Waxflower
Genista	Lilac		

March

Acacia	Ginger	Lilac	Sweet Pea
Amaryllis	Heather	Lily of the Valley	Sweet William
Anemone	Heliconia	Lysimachia	Tuberose
Astilbe	Hyacinth	Narcissus	Tulip
Bird of Paradise	Hydrangea	Ranunculus	Viburnum
Daffodil	Ixia	Scabiosa	Waxflower
Genista	Leptospermum		

April

Allium	Genista	Leptospermum	Sweet Pea
Amaryllis	Ginger	Lily of the Valley	Sweet William
Anemone	Godetia	Lysimachia	Trachelium
Astilbe	Heliconia	Monkshood	Tuberose
Bird of Paradise	Hyacinth	Peony	Tulip
Cornflower	Hydrangea	Ranunculus	Viburnum
Daffodil	Ixia	Scabiosa	Waxflower

May

Agapanthus	Cornflower	Lilac	Sweet William
Allium	Feverfew	Lily of the Valley	Trachelium
Amaryllis	Genista	Lysimachia	Tuberose
Anemone	Ginger	Monkshood	Tulip
Astilbe	Godetia	Peony	Viburnum
Belladonna, Amaryllis	Heliconia	Ranunculus	Waxflower
Bird of Paradise	Hydrangea	Scabiosa	Yarrow
Brodiaea	Ixia	Sweet Pea	Zinnia
Campanula	Leptospermum		

June

Agapanthus	Campanula	Ixia	Sunflower
Allium	Candytuft	Leptospermum	Sweet Pea
Amaranthus	Cornflower	Lysimachia	Sweet William
Aster, China	Crocosmia	Monkshood	Trachelium
Astilbe	Feverfew	Peony	Tuberose
Belladonna, Amaryllis	Godetia	Physostegia	Yarrow
Bird of Paradise	Hydrangea	Scabiosa	Zinnia
Brodiaea			

15

July

Agapanthus	Brodiaea	Godetia	Sunflower
Allium	Campanula	Hydrangea	Sweet Pea
Amaranthus	Candytuft	Ixia	Sweet William
Aster, China	Cornflower	Lysimachia	Trachelium
Astilbe	Crocosmia	Monkshood	Tuberose
Belladonna, Amaryllis	Dahlia	Physostegia	Yarrow
Bird of Paradise	Feverfew	Scabiosa	Zinnia

August

Agapanthus	Campanula	Hydrangea	Sweet Pea
Allium	Candytuft	Ixia	Sweet William
Amaranthus	Cornflower	Lysimachia	Trachelium
Aster, China	Crocosmia	Monkshood	Tuberose
Astilbe	Dahlia	Physostegia	Yarrow
Belladonna, Amaryllis	Feverfew	Scabiosa	Zinnia
Brodiaea	Godetia	Sunflower	

September

Allium	Campanula	Heliconia	Sunflower
Amaranthus	Cornflower	Hydrangea	Sweet William
Amaryllis	Crocosmia	Leptospermum	Trachelium
Aster, China	Dahlia	Lysimachia	Tuberose
Astilbe	Feverfew	Monkshood	Tulip
Belladonna, Amaryllis	Ginger	Physostegia	Yarrow
Bird of Paradise	Godetia	Scabiosa	Zinnia
Brodiaea			

October

Acacia	Dahlia	Leptospermum	Sunflower
Amaranthus	Feverfew	Lysimachia	Sweet William
Amaryllis	Ginger	Monkshood	Tuberose
Anemone	Godetia	Physostegia	Tulip
Belladonna, Amaryllis	Hydrangea	Scabiosa	Zinnia
Bird of Paradise			

November

Acacia	Bird of Paradise	Leptospermum	Physostegia
Amaryllis	Ginger	Lilac	Scabiosa
Anemone	Heather	Lysimachia	Sweet William
Astilbe	Hyacinth	Monkshood	Tulip
Belladonna, Amaryllis	Hydrangea	Narcissus	

December

Acacia	Daffodil	Leptospermum	Narcissus
Amaryllis	Ginger	Lilac	Scabiosa
Anemone	Heather	Lily of the Valley	Sweet William
Astilbe	Hyacinth	Monkshood	Tulip
Bird of Paradise	Hydrangea		

FLOWERS FOR

Your

WEDDING

Bouquet

The wedding style you choose will influence the style of bouquet that you select. If you are planning the ultimate formal evening wedding, your elegant dress will feature a long train and it will be complemented by a long veil. Your flowers should reflect this high style. A fuller, flowing cascade or an arching, crescent-style bouquet are excellent choices. Similar styles work well if this wedding is planned for the daytime, when you might want to consider an opulent, round-style bouquet. A prayer book decorated in delicate flowers is suitable for any dress or wedding style and holds fond memories as well.

If you are planning a traditional formal wedding, your dress will feature a train of some length and a veil that complements your dress. The full and flowing bouquets described above are quite appropriate for this event. If your formal wedding is planned for the daytime, your dress may be the same as for a formal evening wedding, or it may be shorter with a detachable train. Your veil should complement your dress, or you might opt for a hat. The bouquet you choose for your formal daytime wedding is similar to the one for a formal evening wedding — beautiful and elegant, a reflection of the day.

A long or short dress style is appropriate if you plan to have a semiformal evening wedding. A train on your dress is optional, and the veil you select should coordinate with the style of your dress. Less formal bouquet styles are appropriate. A carefree round bouquet of roses or a delicate cascade of mixed flowers will create just the right look. If you want a simple look, opt for a single flower styling or simple clutch bouquet. For a semiformal daytime wedding, select a simple dress with style, perhaps in a pastel color. Add a short veil to complement the look, with a smaller bouquet in any style to complete it.

For the informal wedding, a suit or dress with coordinated accessories is appropriate.

Smaller bouquet styles work best, with single flower stylings popular as well as flowers that coordinate with the location of the wedding.

If you have selected a unique theme or location for your wedding, be sure to select attire that is appropriate for the ceremony. The flowers you choose should also reflect the style and carry out the theme.

Beautiful bouquets, carried with style, enhance the captivating look of the bridal and attendants' gowns.

While the style and time of your wedding are two important factors in determining the style of your bouquet, another and probably the most important is you. Select a bouquet style that flatters your figure as well as your dress and personality. Your bouquet should be proportioned to complement your size. If you are petite you can still have the flowing cascade bouquet you have dreamed of, provided that it is styled proportional to your figure. If you are tall, you can select a fuller bouquet style because you have the presence to carry it.

Selecting your bouquet is a reflection of your personal taste. Be sure to choose something you like, as the flowers you carry as you walk down the aisle will be one of your fondest memories of the day.

Carrying Your Bouquet

Bouquets should be carried gracefully. The bouquet style and features of the gown will influence the way a bouquet should be carried. Bouquets held in front should be low enough to reveal beautiful details of the gown. Hold with both hands as if the arms were resting on the hips. This is the way to hold cascade bouquets, most round-style bouquets and crescent bouquets. The natural tendency when excited is to bring the bouquet to your waist or higher; try to avoid this so that everyone can see the beauty of your gown.

A bouquet can be held to the side with one hand at the same level as a bouquet held in front. This carrying method is effective only if the bouquet is delicate and lightweight, and will work well with small nosegays, clutch bouquets and single flower stylings. Arm bouquets should rest naturally in the crook of the arm so that the flowers face away from the body. Specialty bouquets such as prayer books, fans or baskets should be carried according to size. Smaller specialty bouquets can be carried to the front or side, while larger baskets are usually carried down and to the side. Whatever style of bouquet you choose, remember to carry it in the appropriate way so that you will look beautiful and graceful as you walk down the aisle.

Bouquet Styles and Flowers to Wear

The vision of you as a bride walking down the aisle would not be complete without your bridal bouquet. The look and feeling that flowers add to this moment cannot be described. The flower bouquets your attendants carry as well as the beautiful flowers given to members of the family and special honored guests to wear will all contribute to this special moment.

Here you will find an introduction to the various bouquet styles and flowers to wear that are available for you to choose from. The many colorful photos filled with enticing floral looks and detailed descriptions will allow you to begin to explore your possibilities — and this is only the beginning. Select a shape, change a color, combine different flowers, let your imagination take flight! With the guidance and experience of your professional floral consultant, you can create the wedding flowers of your dreams.

Cascade

BOUQUETS

This delicate combination of peach roses, champagne sweetheart roses, miniature carnations and alstroemeria takes on a romantic feeling. Lacy plumosa foliage cascades down and provides a delicate accent to the flowers in this bouquet. The soft coloring of these flowers will accent many color themes including peach, teal, white and ivory, and purple. The flowers in this bouquet come in a beautiful array of natural colors that can be used as alternatives to complement any color theme.

The cascade bouquet is a traditional favorite with brides because of its full, flowing appearance. This elegant styling is usually carried by the bride, but is also popular for attendants when the bride wants a formal or sophisticated look. Cascade bouquets are a dramatic accent for elegant bridal fashion. This distinctive bouquet style includes an abundance of flowers at the top of the bouquet, gracefully combined with a cascade of flowers, delicate foliage or ribbon streamers. Cascade bouquets should be proportioned to the size of the bride and her gown to create the ultimate floral accent.

A classic cascade bouquet is styled with gardenias and stephanotis. Fragrant blossoms and elegant design make this bouquet perfect for the most formal of weddings. Variegated ivy softens the overall look and can be clipped from the bouquet after the ceremony and grown for a lasting memory.

Soft colors and delicate foliage accent this cascade bouquet. Pale lavender freesia, peach roses and purple delphinium are intermixed with beautiful white roses and stephanotis to create this elegant look. A soft accent of color can dramatically change a traditional all-white bouquet into a wonderful color accent.

This stylish cascade bouquet combines the romantic look of pink and white roses with the graceful gerbera daisy. Miniature carnations and bouvardia add the finishing touch. Delicate plumosa foliage accents the entire bouquet. The perfect accent for pink or teal color themes, this bouquet can be recreated with many other natural color flowers.

A striking triad of color is formed by using lush peach and purple flowers combined with delicate green foliage. The cascade styling of this bouquet offers a fuller, flowing look. The bouquet features miniature gerbera daisies, peach roses, violet stock and purple scabiosa, delphinium and freesia. This bouquet is a natural for a peach or purple color theme wedding and a striking complement for teal.

White roses and freesia, together with soft pink miniature carnations, form a romantic combination of flowers. The cascade bouquet is styled with a delicate arching effect, and the lacy look of the bouquet is created by tiny gypsophila blossoms and variegated ivy. The coloring of this bouquet accents any number of wedding color themes and can easily be altered to complement others. Changing the carnations to white makes this bouquet a traditional all-white bridal bouquet.

21

Round
BOUQUETS

This round-style bouquet features roses in shades of champagne, pink and peach. Gerbera daisies and a touch of cream stock are added to enhance the look. The spilling flowers and trailing ivy accent in the lower portion of the bouquet provide an interesting shape, with the ivy treatment also adding movement to this lush cluster of flowers. This is an elegant choice for a bride who prefers color in her bouquet.

This beautiful bride is holding a bouquet styled with a delicate combination of alstroemeria, Queen Anne's lace, freesia, tulips, roses and scabiosa. The natural look of this bouquet is complemented by rich ivy foliage that moves freely below the flowers.

Traditional, round-style bouquets are popular with brides and their attendants. This simple but elegant styling, also called the colonial bouquet, is suitable for formal or informal weddings. Nosegay and Biedermeier are other names referring to round-style bouquets. A nosegay is usually a small cluster of flowers formed in a round shape, while the European-influenced Biedermeier consists of individual blossoms placed in concentric circles within the bouquet.

Round-style bouquets can be created with simple combinations of one or two flowers or with a multitude of flower varieties. Flowers can be formed into tight clusters or loosely arranged in freeform styles, and although the name suggests a round form, the bouquet does not have to be perfectly round in shape. The flowers included in a round-style bouquet will influence the formality of the bouquet. A bouquet styled with more formal flowers like gardenias and stephanotis will take on a more sophisticated look, while simple carnations and daisies create a casual look.

Round-style bouquets can vary in size from large to small, but like the cascade bouquet, they should be proportional in size to the person who will be carrying it.

The delicate combination of champagne and sonia roses, peach lilies and white stock creates the look of romance in this round-style bouquet. The sheer white ribbon treatment and dainty Queen Anne's lace accent the other flowers, fashioning a lovely bouquet. The colors of this bouquet are perfect for a green, peach or teal color scheme.

This Biedermeier-style bouquet features vibrant blossoms in a defined circular pattern. The rich blue-violet combination of delphinium, cornflowers and statice with electric red carnations, all centered by a classic red rose, creates an impressive bouquet. The green foliage placed throughout the bouquet in the same circular pattern enhances the striking color.

Vibrant colors create excitement in this beautiful mixed flower bouquet. Roses, gerbera daisies, alstroemeria, asters, waxflower, pompons and carnations in various colors are just some of the flowers used to style this look. This striking combination is suitable for almost any color theme.

A sheer ribbon treatment provides a soft accent to this enchanting bouquet. The look features roses, stock, snapdragons, gerbera daisies and purple lisianthus blossoms. This bouquet nicely accents green, purple or peach color themes.

23

Crescent
BOUQUETS

Romance is in the air with this delicate crescent bouquet styled in softer, pastel colors. "Le Reve" lily blossoms are surrounded by pink roses, miniature carnations and dainty waxflower. The calathea leaves with a light pink stripe add to the beauty of this bouquet. The look of this bouquet would be perfect for the bride in an informal wedding or would grace the appearance of the bridal attendants.

Crescent bouquets provide a dramatic look for today's bride. The crescent-shaped bouquet features an arching form, with flowers extending out from the center of the bouquet. The unique styling look of crescent bouquets can range from traditional to contemporary.

The shape of a crescent bouquet will vary depending on the flowers used and the desired look. Two distinctive forms are typically associated with crescent bouquets. A symmetrical crescent bouquet features arching flower garlands of the same length, creating a balanced look.

The asymmetrical crescent bouquet features a garland on one side longer than the garland on the other side. Crescent bouquets can be created in large or small sizes, with flowers arching from left to right or right to left depending on preference. The elegant look of the crescent bouquet is a graceful floral enhancement.

Cattleya orchids form the center of this crescent bouquet. The crescent shape is created with sprays of dendrobium orchids, bridal white roses and freesia. Lush green ivy completes the look. This bouquet is an elegant choice for a formal wedding in a cathedral or a larger, older-style church.

A classic white crescent bouquet features a trail of white roses, cymbidium orchids and fragrant stephanotis. The addition of the delicate stephanotis blossoms, which stand for "Happiness in Marriage" in the language of flowers, gives symbolic meaning to the bouquet. The decorative foliage provides the arching form and the flowers complete the crescent shape.

A striking combination of color and shape is represented in this crescent bouquet. The clustering of vibrant red gerbera daisies, burgundy carnations, red amaranthus and cream roses tipped with red creates the center of the bouquet, while sprays of purple dendrobium orchids and fragrant eucalyptus complete the shape. The coloring in this bouquet is perfect for a wedding that is planned in jeweltones.

A unique triad of colors makes an interesting crescent bouquet perfect for a yellow color scheme, as well as other color themes including purple and green. This striking bouquet includes red and yellow roses, yellow snap dragons, yellow daisy pompons, lavender freesia, purple asters, purple larkspur, caspia and agapanthus florets. Ivy strands descend from the flowers clustered in the center, forming the crescent line.

A violet wedding color scheme can be complemented with this crescent bouquet. A variety of foliage textures provides the arching background in this stunning bouquet. White cymbidium orchids are encircled with lavender roses, lavender miniature carnations and physostegia to create this traditional crescent bouquet style. The coloring in this bouquet complements a violet wedding color scheme, but can easily be adapted to enhance many others.

25

Rose
BOUQUETS

Vibrant red roses are clustered into a classically round bouquet. The plaid ribbon accent makes this bouquet perfect for a holiday or winter wedding. A quick change of the ribbon gives the bouquet a whole new look. For a more delicate bouquet, try combining pink roses with a sheer ribbon to coordinate.

A traditional favorite is the arm bouquet of roses. This hand-tied bouquet features bright pink roses and lush foliage accented with a coordinating bow. The simple styling of this bouquet is versatile and can be recreated with different colors of roses and ribbon to create just the right look.

There is nothing more enchanting than a rose. Roses are traditional flowers symbolizing love and romance. They are beautiful, fragrant and can be styled to create just the right look for all types of weddings. Roses are gorgeous and always the popular flower choice for bridal bouquets.

The selection of roses is almost unending and continues to grow each year. There are hundreds of rose varieties to choose from in many sizes and a rainbow of colors. From traditional red, white, pink and yellow to shades of lavender, peach and bicolor varieties, there is a rose available to enhance every wedding color theme.

Roses symbolize many different meanings within the language of flowers. Depending on the color or variety of the rose, it can represent love, beauty, grace, devotion and many other feelings and emotions. Select a rose for your bouquet by its meaning or simply because of its beautiful color. Whether you select an elaborate bouquet, a smaller cluster or a hand-tied look, choosing roses will allow you to create a most extraordinary bouquet for your wedding day.

A distinctive color triad is formed with beautiful peach and lavender roses and rich green foliage in this cascading bouquet. A delicate statice accents the look. This bouquet complements a variety of wedding color themes including peach, lavender and green.

Delicate peach roses accented with variegated ivy are clustered into this unique shape for a simple but striking look. White satin ribbon is added to coordinate with the variegation in the ivy. To create a fuller appearance, the roses are allowed to open before the bouquet is made. The soft coloring of this bouquet will complement many color schemes, or style with different color roses if you prefer.

Simple elegance is represented by this stunning, hand-tied rose bouquet. Beautiful long-stemmed roses are carefully placed at precise intervals and tied with a splendid tulle bow. The roses are accented with distinctive variegated ivy, creating a sophisticated look for attendants to carry. For yet a different flower look for your attendants, place long-stemmed roses loosely in a gathering basket and accent with a soft bow.

This charming, heart-shaped bouquet features champagne sweetheart roses clustered into shape, then surrounded by white bouvardia to provide a delicate outline effect. The bouquet is accented with a sheer gold ribbon. This romantic bouquet style offers a fresh alternative to traditional shapes. Heart-shaped bouquets can be carried by the bride, bridesmaids, or flower girls.

27

Arm
BOUQUETS AND
SINGLE FLOWERS
TO CARRY

A practical alternative to a formal bridal bouquet is an arm bouquet or single flower styled to carry. The arm bouquet is created by gathering flowers together in a loose fashion and tying with a coordinating ribbon accent. This bouquet style is popular with the bride who prefers a natural look for herself or her attendants, and is most popular for informal weddings. If you are planning a formal wedding and like this style, there are many ways you can dress up the look with the flowers, foliage or ribbon you select. Arm bouquets can be styled with as few as one or two flowers or with many elegant flower varieties combined into an impressive display.

Single flowers to carry are usually made with flowers that lend themselves to individual presentations, such as flowers that grow naturally on a spray, one or two single flowers with strong visual presence or a composite flower. Many elegant orchids including dendrobium, phalaenopsis and cymbidium grow naturally on sprays that can be used to create a simple but beautiful look. Gardenias, cattleya and japhet orchids, gerbera daisies and even some varieties of roses are excellent choices of flowers with the visual presence to be carried individually in a small presentation. A composite flower is one that has been expanded in size and beauty, with petals added to the original flower to create an enhanced look. These various styles of simple flowers to carry are usually light and airy and are normally carried at more informal weddings. However, depending on the flowers you choose, there are many single flower variations that are appropriate for formal affairs.

From natural expressions to elegant floral presentations, arm bouquets and single flower stylings offer many options for today's bride.

The arm bouquets carried by the bride and her attendant in this photo reflect a classic look. Calla lilies form a lavish presentation, with a tight cluster of bicolor roses accenting the base of the bouquet. The foliage accent establishes a background for the simple form of the callas. The similarity between the bride's and the attendant's bouquets gives the ceremony a harmonious look, as the same flowers are used in each bouquet with the bride typically carrying the larger one.

An extraordinary phalaenopsis orchid spray is surrounded with sheer white ribbon to create this unique look. This arm bouquet is suitable for any style wedding because of its casual but elegant charm.

White casablanca lilies are tied with shimmering silver ribbon to style this simple arm bouquet. The variegated ivy cascades from the lilies to add size and movement to the bouquet. The exquisite nature of the pure white lilies complements any color theme, or you may change the lily to another variety to add color.

This beautiful bouquet appears to be one large single flower, but in reality it is a composite flower called a glamellia. A glamellia is created by combining individual gladiolus blossoms to form this unique flower, which is then backed with striking foliage to complete the look.

Lavish cymbidium orchids designed for your attendant's wrist present a stylish alternative to traditional bouquet styles. The orchids are enhanced with a simple strand of ivy and lavender ribbon, creating a sophisticated look for an afternoon wedding.

A trio of pink gerbera daisies is tied together to give the appearance of a single flower. Ribbon crisscrosses the stems with a full satin bow tied at the base of the flowers. This stunning presentation for an informal wedding can be recreated in any number of vivid colors.

This hand-tied bouquet is ideal for an informal wedding. Just picture your bridesmaids carrying this in your spring or summertime wedding. The bouquet is styled with a delicate mixture of cream-colored gerbera daisies, carnations and delphinium. Astilbe, asters and roses complement the look. The finishing touch is provided by the lacy foliage and multiple ribbon textures. This bouquet can be created in any number of flower varieties and colors.

29

Specialty

BOUQUETS

*I*f you are looking for different and unique, the specialty-style bouquet is for you. This bouquet styling is popular with the bride who wants her wedding flowers to be distinctive or who is trying to achieve an individualized look. There are many types of specialty-style bouquets including fans, parasols, wreaths, baskets, pomander balls and candle accents. Fans and parasols take on many forms and can be easily decorated with flowers to complement the look of your wedding. Many wreath styles can be created with foliage, foliage and flowers or delicate branches formed into a wreath shape, with flowers added to soften the look. Depending on the style of the basket you select, basket bouquets can help you express a variety of wedding themes. From a small painted basket to a larger gathering basket, you can create an enchanting look. The pomander ball is one of the most dramatic-looking specialty bouquet styles. A pomander ball is made by covering a sphere shape with many blossoms or petals. You can carry just one pomander ball or combine two or three to intensify the dramatic look. Romantic candlelight can be added to attendants' bouquets by using a glass-covered candleholder as the base of the bouquet. Be sure to check on this before ordering, as local fire regulations may prohibit the carrying of open flames.

While the use of specialty-style bouquets is always a delightful way to add flowers to your wedding, accenting a prayer book with delicate flowers makes a particularly meaningful bouquet. Carry a prayer book that is a gift from a special friend, your groom's family heirloom, or the same book your mother carried in her wedding — whatever fond memory the prayer book offers, you will make it a lasting one by adding a beautiful accent of flowers.

Whether a specialty-style bouquet is right for you will depend on the style of your wedding and your personality. By selecting a unique bouquet, you will add your own personal touch to your wedding flowers.

Uphold family tradition or start a new one by carrying a prayer book decorated with a small accent of flowers. Select delicate flowers for the top or open the book to your favorite passage and place the flowers there. Your florist can offer many other suggestions for using prayer books and other keepsake items in your bouquet. This prayer book is accented with fragrant gardenias and exquisite gold ribbon.

A bouquet accented with candlelight is romantic for an evening wedding. This bouquet features a crystal goblet surrounded by pink and cream bicolor sweetheart roses and pink miniature carnations. The elegant ribbon completes the look. An engraved goblet will become a treasured gift for your attendants. Be sure to check on any restrictions on the use of candles at your wedding ceremony.

A small Bible is included in this bouquet featuring white spray roses, bridal pink roses, alstroemeria and stephanotis. A ribbon accent trails below with strands of ivy, creating a delicate look. The dainty feeling of the bouquet is enhanced by the tiny pearls placed in each stephanotis blossom.

Carried on a ribbon handle, the pomander ball makes a stunning statement. This globe-shaped floral display can be styled with one or many types of flowers. You can carry one, two or even three floral spheres of the same or varying size. Here, a dramatic duo of pomander balls is shown. Perfect for a jeweltone color scheme, this bouquet uses a variety of mixed flowers including roses, asters, delphinium, statice, carnations, phlox, lisianthus and alstroemeria, all in vibrant colors.

A lovely Victorian lace fan accented with white satin ribbon, peach roses and spray roses is a wonderful alternative to a traditional bouquet. Delicate maidenhair fern complements the lacy look of the fan and provides the finishing touch.

Basket bouquets are popular for informal outdoor weddings. The basket can also serve as a decorative keepsake for your attendants after the wedding. This delightful basket of roses, freesia, iris, alstroemeria, statice and Queen Anne's lace is complemented with ivy strands.

Basket bouquets can be styled in any size basket, depending on your preference. This elegant gold basket features white casablanca lilies, blue delphinium, light yellow roses, nigella, asters and Queen Anne's lace. A full bow accenting the front of the basket coordinates with the attendant's dress. This beautiful basket of flowers can also be placed in a special location at the reception to further enhance your decorations.

31

Contemporary

FREEFORM BOUQUETS

*I*f you are a bride willing to step outside of traditional looks into contemporary, then freeform bouquet styles are for you. Interesting shapes, uncommon flower varieties and anything unique are the fashion. Contemporary freeform bouquet styles are modern interpretations of some of the traditional favorites like cascade or crescent bouquets. Trailing flowers and arching lines are common to this style as well as abstract round shapes. If you like tropical flowers with interesting shapes such as anthurium, bird of paradise or protea, a contemporary presentation is a natural way to style them. Traditional popular wedding flowers such as orchids, roses and even mixed flowers can be styled into interesting modern shapes.

If you prefer the nontraditional look for flowers at your wedding, then freeform bouquets may be the answer. By working closely with your florist you will be able to create a contemporary freeform bouquet that reflects your personal style.

A striking mixture of flowers is presented in freeform style. The vibrant red, yellow and orange flowers are accented with blue cornflowers. Nephthytis and galax leaves form the background, with sprengeri and bear grass adding a delicate finishing touch.

This contemporary bouquet features colorful bird of paradise and dramatic foliage with distinctive orange berries and sponge mushrooms providing an exotic focal point. Bird of paradise stems are added to balance the visual look of the bouquet.

The extraordinary shape of the anthurium flower is featured in this contemporary bouquet. Foliage with interesting color variations and textures provides an interesting accent while allium adds a touch of color. This contemporary bouquet conveys the essence of a traditional cascade bouquet.

Contemporary styling is combined with the features of a traditional cascade bouquet to form this exquisite bouquet. White calla lilies and clustered white roses are used to create the top of the bouquet with additional callas suspended below.

Elegant phalaenopsis orchids with their graceful form and vibrant color are styled into this contemporary bouquet. The orchids are clustered with nephthytis leaves to form the top of the bouquet while a smaller coordinating accent moves freely below.

This enchanting look features magnificently colored roses and bouvardia blossoms. Oncidium orchid sprays cascade from the bouquet, creating a waterfall effect.

33

Different
BOUQUETS CREATED
WITH THE SAME FLOWER

Many different floral looks can be created using the same flower. From traditional to contemporary, elaborate to simple, the variety of looks that can be created with the same flower is remarkable. In addition, these same bouquets also take on an entirely different look when you change the flower color, add interesting foliage or accent with your favorite ribbon — your options are endless. Featured here are two examples of exciting but very different looks using the same flower in different bouquet styles. Three distinctive bouquets are created with delicate peach gerbera daisies and alstroemeria and three with fragrant gardenias to illustrate the different looks you can achieve. If you have a favorite flower in mind but haven't decided on bouquet style, your florist will be able to help you determine the right kind of bouquet for your wedding theme and budget.

A cluster of peach gerbera daisies and peach alstroemeria is formed into a clutch-style bouquet for a different look. Perfect for a garden wedding, this bouquet can be created in any of the rainbow of colors that these flowers are available in. Maidenhair fern and satin ribbon provide the finishing touch.

In this bouquet the two flower varieties are styled in classic cascade form. The peach gerbera daisies are surrounded by alstroemeria and maidenhair fern to create an opulent look. This elegant cascade bouquet will enhance your peach wedding color scheme or you can change the color to complement the color theme of your choice.

A trio of peach gerbera daisies is surrounded by alstroemeria to create this contemporary crescent bouquet. Striking calathea leaves combined with spider plant foliage help shape the bouquet. This bouquet complements a teal, green or peach wedding color scheme.

A colonial bouquet styled with fragrant gardenias and white spray roses is a classic bridal bouquet. The white satin ribbon adds a touch of elegance.

Gardenias are exquisite when featured in simple presentations. Beautiful white satin ribbon is looped to form a handle and then accented with a gardenia and white spray roses. This elegant display is suitable for a second marriage or bridal attendant.

Two gardenias and white satin ribbon form a petite clutch bouquet. This bouquet is an excellent selection for an informal wedding or a tasteful choice for a second marriage. Lush green ivy strands accent this elegant, fragrant bouquet.

Clutch
BOUQUETS

The beautiful clutch-style bouquet combines the form of a round-style bouquet with the simple presentation of an arm or tied bouquet. The clutch bouquet style is growing in popularity because the look is simple but elegant, and can be carried by the bride or her attendants. This style features simple combinations of flowers clustered in an upright fashion. The stems of these clustered flowers can be wrapped with ribbon or cording, or left plain if you prefer. Clutch bouquets can be styled in various sizes depending on your preference; however, most are smaller than traditional bridal bouquets.

Delicate white and yellow blossoms are combined in this lovely clutch bouquet. The bouquet is styled with yellow roses, white roses, star of Bethlehem, white miniature carnations and yellow daisy pompons. Variegated ivy forms a collar at the base of the flowers and white cording covers the stems to complete the look.

This natural-looking clutch bouquet is perfect for a wedding in white or ivory, or other wedding color themes such as pink, teal or violet. Created by hand-tying the flowers into the clutch form, the bouquet features bells of Ireland, white lisianthus, miniature carnations, yellow sweetheart roses, pale yellow roses, green amaranthus and white sweetheart roses. A sheer metallic ribbon completes the look.

The pink and purple gingham-checked ribbon gives this clutch bouquet a whimsical, festive look. It accents a cluster of miniature carnation blossoms in a multitude of colors. Although the vibrant pink, lavender and yellow colors make this bouquet suitable for any number of color themes, it is especially suited for a spring or summer-time wedding.

This vibrant cluster of flowers can complement any number of color schemes from black to purple or pink. Bells of Ireland, roses, larkspur, hydrangea blossoms, carnations and statice are combined to create this versatile clutch bouquet. To change the color emphasis of the bouquet, switch the purple ribbon to a different color.

A bounty of open garden roses is clustered into this romantic clutch-style bouquet. Variegated pittosporum leaves are tucked between the roses to enhance the look. The simple styling is accented with yellow satin ribbon braided to cover the stems. This bouquet is perfect for attendants in an afternoon wedding.

A cherished moment with your flower girl features a romantic clutch bouquet. Elegant ribbon forms a beautiful background for the delicate mix of pastel flowers in this clutch bouquet. A subtle combination of white and pink roses, champagne and pink sweetheart roses, soft peach roses, pink and lavender stock and lavender pompons is included in this charming bouquet. A smaller version is perfect for your flower girl to carry. For an extra touch, coordinate a floral hairpiece with your bouquet.

37

Flowers

FOR CHILDREN TO CARRY

One way to make your wedding memorable is to include the warmth and innocence of children who are special to you and your fiancé. You can invite any number of small children to participate as flower girls and ring bearers. Whether you include one flower girl or several children, their spirit and charm will create a treasured memory.

The flowers you select for the children should coordinate with the flowers you have selected for yourself and your attendants. There are many floral accents that are perfect for children to carry. The choice for flower girls includes small nosegay or clutch-style bouquets, baskets filled with flowers or loose petals, wreaths, pomander balls and garlands. Any small floral accent is suitable for a child to carry. Be sure to include coordinating flowers for the hair. For ring bearers a satin or lace pillow for the rings, accented with flowers, is appropriate. A small boutonniere for the lapel of the ring bearer's jacket completes the look.

Flowers for the children in your wedding should be proportional to the size of the child so they are easy to hold and do not overpower the child. The flowers should not be styled too large for them to handle as they walk down the aisle. If you are using several children, you can create a captivating look by varying the style of flowers that each child carries. Styling in soft colors and adding a bit of ribbon or lace to complement the children's outfit or wedding color scheme will add to the look of innocence.

This ring bearer's pillow accented with pink and lavender flowers and pink tulle creates a charming look. Flowers include pink sweetheart roses, lavender miniature carnations and lavender waxflower. Be sure to include a pink sweetheart rose boutonniere for the lapel.

A delicate look is created for this ring bearer's pillow accented with peach alstroemeria, miniature carnations and bronze button pompons. Maidenhair fern accents the flowers while a combination of ribbons with different textures coordinates with the pillow.

A complementary wreath for the flower girl is a delightful flower style for a child to carry. This dainty wreath features peach alstroemeria, Queen Anne's lace, peach spray roses and champagne sweetheart roses. Variegated ivy softens the look, and peach cording continues the color theme.

The fairy-tale look of this flower girl's nosegay is enchanting. Styled with delicate pink flowers, this nosegay coordinates with the ring bearer's pillow. Soft pink tulle surrounds pink sweetheart roses, lavender miniature carnations and lavender waxflower, creating a delicate cluster of flowers.

A lovely flower girl's basket decorated with mixed flowers and variegated ivy is a charming way to carry rose petals down the aisle. The edge of the basket is trimmed with yellow roses, lavender freesia, caspia, lavender asters, miniature carnation blossoms and pompons.

Mixed flowers accent this ivory satin ring bearer's pillow to coordinate with the trimmed flower girl's basket. Variegated ivy is the background for a yellow rose, miniature carnation blossom, lavender freesia, lavender aster, caspia and white pompons, creating a dainty look.

A nosegay of cheerful yellow flowers accented with sheer white and yellow ribbon is the perfect choice for a flower girl. This nosegay features yellow spray roses, freesia, button and daisy pompons, statice and miniature carnations. It can be styled in a number of colors to complement many different wedding color schemes.

A coordinating ring bearer's pillow is created using flowers similar to the flower girl's bouquet and a heart-shaped pillow. Included are yellow stock blossoms, sweetheart roses and daisy pompons with strands of green ivy to enhance the floral display.

39

Sonia roses are clustered into a hairpiece that beautifully accents this French twist hair style. This elegant look is perfect for bridal attendants or a bride in an informal wedding. By changing the color of the rose, you can create a style suitable for any wedding color scheme.

A beautiful bridal headpiece is styled with white flowers attached to a veil. This headpiece features stephanotis, white dendrobium orchid blossoms and a white rose. White bridal ribbon, cording and a touch of variegated ivy provide the finishing touch.

Shimmery white and gold ribbon enhances a single phalaenopsis orchid. This stylish hairpiece is suitable for a bride or her attendants. The hairpiece coordinates with an exquisite spray of phalaenopsis orchids tied with the same shimmery ribbons. This elegant look is appropriate for almost any style wedding.

Another way to add the beauty and grace of flowers to the fashion look of your wedding day is with floral hairpieces. Flowers in the hair form a natural complement to the bouquet you select for yourself and your attendants. Whether you choose a floral hairpiece as an accent for your attendants, flower girls or yourself, there are many styles to choose from. Flowers in the hair can be placed at the side or back of the head, on top as a headband, or as a floral wreath or crown that rests on top of the head. A veil or ribbons may also be attached to the floral hairpiece to complement the look. Floral hairpieces are easily secured in your hair with pins and combs, or simply tuck loose flowers into styled hair.

Flowers for the hair should be styled in a delicate fashion, and should coordinate with the flowers and coloring of the bouquets you have selected. If you opt for a traditional veil for the wedding ceremony, you can remove it at the reception and replace it with a beautiful floral hairpiece. Flowers are a perfect complement for your attendants' and flower girl's hair. By adding a tailored bow or many streamers you can create just the right look. If you select a stylish hat for your attendants, adorn it with flowers to soften the look. Floral hairpieces add the finishing touch to the fashions you have so carefully chosen for your wedding day.

This stylish attendant's hat is accented with a delicate mix of garden flowers. This striking look is suitable for an afternoon summer wedding and coordinates nicely with a floral print dress. The hat is accented with a lavender rose, lavender scabiosa, pink astilbe, stock florets and blue agapanthus florets. The floral accent on the hat is styled to coordinate with the beautiful bouquet the attendant is holding.

Braided hair is beautifully accented with mixed flowers placed in the hair with bobby pins. The lovely floral look includes stephanotis, light peach roses and pink sweetheart roses. The porcelain appearance of the flowers is created with special pearlized floral paint. Consult your florist for further suggestions on ways to enhance flowers and create special looks.

A striking bridal look is created by adding this vibrant colored rose and alstroemeria floral accent to a simple veil. The lush ivy accentuates the rich tones of the red sweetheart roses, yellow spray roses and orange alstroemeria blossoms. This look is perfect for a fall wedding.

A formal black and white wedding color scheme is accented with this vibrant flower mix in shades of peach and red. A floral hairpiece for the side of the head complements the attendant's bouquet, creating this exquisite look. The groomsman's boutonniere also coordinates. Flowers used to create this stunning combination include roses, leptospermum, spray roses, miniature carnations and yarrow.

41

Corsages

AND
BOUTONNIERES

AND
BOUTONNIERES

This unique round-style corsage features small pink roses, daisy pompons, blue delphinium blossoms, cornflowers and white miniature carnations. Lavender satin ribbon completes the look. Coordinating blossoms form a striking boutonniere.

Flowers to wear in the form of corsages and boutonnieres are cherished floral accents for the parents, grandparents, special guests and others taking part in your wedding. Corsages and boutonnieres can be styled in a variety of sizes, colors, shapes and flower types. They are usually designed to coordinate with other wedding flowers in variety and color.

Corsage-style floral accents are appropriate for the special women taking part in your wedding. Mothers and grandmothers who are attending should be honored with a special corsage. You should also consider giving a floral tribute to recognize other special guests including special aunts and godmothers, and to distinguish the women assisting with the ceremony or reception such as readers, guest book attendant and hostess. Corsages are an important part of the wedding because they not only recognize important members of your and your fiancé's families, but they also say thank you to your friends who are working to keep the events of your wedding running smoothly.

The corsage is typically worn on the left shoulder with stems and ribbons down; however, some of the newer contemporary stylings can be worn many different ways. When placed on the shoulder a lovely corsage will enhance the style of the gown with the design of the flowers. Almost any corsage can be adapted into a wrist corsage, which is traditionally worn on the left arm. Floral accents can also be created to be placed at the waist or any other point that will accent the gown. Corsages can also be placed on an evening bag, making a striking accessory when flowers on the gown would be inappropriate because of sheer fabric or style.

A boutonniere is just as important as the corsage in giving recognition to the special people taking part in your wedding. Besides the groom and his groomsmen, fathers, grandfathers and other special male guests should be honored with boutonnieres. Most men prefer to wear a single flower or a small cluster of flowers. Boutonnieres should be worn on the left lapel.

This corsage and boutonniere combination is perfect for a blue or violet wedding color scheme. The boutonniere features a small white rose, purple delphinium blossom and bud accented with ivy leaves. The corsage is styled with white roses and delphinium in shades of purple and lavender. A blending of satin ribbons completes the look.

Mixed pastel flowers are the choice for a spring or summer wedding. This delicate look is created with a small rose and blossoms from lavender freesia and peach alstroemeria, accented with camellia leaves. Dainty gypsophila and soft ribbon add the finishing touch. A cluster of coordinating blossoms forms the boutonniere.

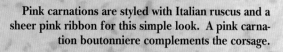

Pink carnations are styled with Italian ruscus and a sheer pink ribbon for this simple look. A pink carnation boutonniere complements the corsage.

This boutonniere styled with a combination of fragrant stephanotis and ivy leaves makes use of flower symbolism. The stephanotis flower stands for "happiness in marriage" and ivy stands for "fidelity." This boutonniere would be suitable for a groom. The coordinating corsage also features stephanotis and ivy. White roses, representing "purity," are added to complete the look.

Combining flowers with different meanings is a special way to share a personal message.

Elegant stephanotis blossoms are pearlized with a touch of floral paint to create this romantic look. The stephanotis flowers are grouped with bouvardia in the boutonniere and accented with ming fern and camellia leaves in the corsage.

Champagne roses and peach spray roses, accented with tree fern and pittosporum leaves, create a delicate mix of color for this boutonniere and corsage. The sheer ribbon that accents the corsage adds a soft, romantic touch to the finished look.

A single sonia rose accented with a touch of plumosa is a simple but elegant choice for a boutonniere. A similar look is created for the coordinating corsage with a single opened rose. Petals are added at the base of the flower to make the blossom bigger. Teal ribbon makes this a perfect complement for a teal or peach wedding. Changing the color of the rose or the ribbon will make this corsage coordinate with other colors.

43

A beautiful white cattleya orchid forms a traditional corsage for mothers and grandmothers. The natural beauty of this flower is accented with a simple ribbon. A white rose surrounded with stephanotis is the perfect complement.

White cymbidium orchids are combined with tree fern and white ribbons to create this classic look. A single white carnation with a hint of tree fern is a tasteful complement.

Dendrobium orchid blossoms accented with variegated spider plant leaves are an elegant choice for a corsage and boutonniere. The vibrant bicolored orchid blossoms complement many color themes including formal black. Dendrobium orchids are also available in solid purple and white to create other interesting looks.

Fragrant gardenias will enhance any wedding with their classic beauty and elegant look. Gardenias offer simple sophistication and a pleasing scent. A corsage can be styled with one or two flowers, depending on the look you are trying to achieve. Boutonnieres are best made with one gardenia flower, as men prefer a simple look.

Ceremony Flowers

Because your wedding ceremony is where the memory of the day begins, you want the setting to be special. Whether you choose a simple chapel, elaborate sanctuary, your favorite spot in your grandmother's garden or some other meaningful location, flowers will enhance the expression of your personal style.

In this section you will find many floral ideas that you can use to build the vision of your wedding ceremony. From elegant church settings displaying any number of floral arrangement ideas to romantic garden looks, these pages are filled with alluring images of magical wedding flowers. Combine these ideas with those of your professional floral consultant and add the individual characteristics of the location of your ceremony to create an unforgettable look.

Church
SETTINGS

A traditional church wedding is filled with ritual and symbolism, and is often held in a setting full of personal meaning. You can enhance this setting with a variety of lush flowers and candelabra to add candlelight or to complement the service.

If your wedding is planned for a grand sanctuary, you might consider large floral displays in the front, with smaller floral accents on the pews leading up to the altar. Adding candlelight will create a romantic atmosphere for an evening ceremony. Decorate the candelabra with a beautiful floral accent. If you have selected an intimate chapel for the ceremony, you can use smaller floral treatments to highlight the special characteristics that first attracted you to this setting.

When you select the reverence of a church setting for your wedding, it is important to follow the guidelines for floral decorations as set forth by the individual church. With so many floral options available you should have little problem creating an enchanting look while still following church regulations. Before you reserve the location of your ceremony, check to see what restrictions there might be on decorations to avoid planning something for your ceremony only to find out that you cannot use it. Churches now have guidelines for flowers on the altar, open flames on candles in candelabra, pew decorations, etc. Your floral consultant may also have helpful information concerning restrictions and suggestions on floral alternatives.

The strong architectural lines of this beautiful stone chapel are accented with a colorful stained glass window. The elegant marble altar is adorned with simple bouquets of delphinium, gerbera daisies, stock, snapdragons and roses. Elegant spiral candelabra with coordinating flowers stand at either side of the altar. The warm aura of candlelight complements the warmth of the rich wood carving behind the altar.

A modern church is filled with a striking display of contemporary floral designs created in a variety of white flowers. Twinkling candlelight creates the background for candle arrangements, kneeling bench and whimsical pew arrangements. Shimmery gold ribbon reflects the glow of the candles. A delicate foliage garland sweeps the wooden rail and foliage plants provide the finishing touch.

Pure white lilies and dendrobium orchids are styled into a flowing pew decoration. This bouquet style is used with a carnation treatment and an accent of white gerbera daisies and anthurium to grace the aisle.

Twin kneeling benches are positioned at an angle and centered with a simple bouquet of white roses, gerbera daisies and rich foliage. An elegant gold ribbon accent spills out of the bouquet.

47

*A*ltar
ARRANGEMENTS

*F*lowers can grace the altar of a church in several ways. You can position one arrangement in the center of the altar. This arrangement can be long and low, larger and fan-shaped or stylized. Two coordinating arrangements that match in style and flowers are also popular on the altar.

Select the altar arrangement style that suits the altar in your church. Altar arrangements should never be designed taller than a cross positioned on or above the altar. Make sure as you are planning for a particular style of arrangement that it does not interfere with religious items normally on the altar. Prior to ordering your flowers, be sure to check with your church to verify which items must stay on the altar and which can be removed.

A beautiful brass cross is surrounded by coordinating altar arrangements. Casablanca lilies, carnations and snapdragons are combined with pompon chrysanthemums and spray asters in various white tones to create this classic look. This flower combination is suitable for any color theme or can be easily recreated in any number of flower colors.

Suitable for any wedding color theme, a beautiful garden flower mixture is arranged in a coordinating vase. The vase is filled with an abundance of flowers, including delphinium, stock, gerbera daisies, lisianthus, roses, larkspur, hydrangea and carnations. Gypsophila and spray asters complete the look. The arrangement is centered between brass candle holders.

A simple centerpiece-style arrangement with a trio of candles is perfect for an informal ceremony. Notice how the trio is repeated with striking star gazer lilies and again with the accent of freesia. This altar arrangement can easily be taken to the reception to provide an extra floral accent.

Unity

CANDLE ARRANGEMENTS

A symbolic part of many ceremonies today is the lighting of the unity candle. The unity candle is positioned in the center of two smaller candles that are traditionally lit by the mothers of the bride and groom as they enter for the ceremony. During the ceremony the bride and groom light separate, smaller candles using the candles lit by their mothers. The bride and groom then light the single candle in the center, signifying the joining or uniting of the two in marriage. In most modern ceremonies, the family candles on each side remain lighted to symbolize that bride and groom remain individuals as well as the partners they have just become in their new marriage.

Peach gerbera daisies styled with carnations and pompons surround a white unity candle. Eucalyptus and sprengeri foliage accent the design. Multicolor ribbons form a bow that provides the finishing touch to this arrangement. This unity candle arrangement will complement a peach or teal wedding with style.

Lush maidenhair fern and sprengeri provide the backdrop for this unity candle display. The candle arrangement is filled with asters, snapdragons, lavender roses and purple statice neatly tied with a lace ribbon. White taper candles, standing side by side, complete the look. Use this color combination for a purple color theme or simply add other jeweltone flowers for an entirely different look.

The lacy look of this unity candle is accented with a simple arrangement of cream-colored carnations and white daisy pompons. Tulle ribbon sparkles among the flowers while striking fern foliage completes the look of the design. This delicate arrangement can also be accented with a touch of color if you want a more coordinated look.

49

Candelabra
SETTINGS

An elegant pair of spiral candelabra adorn opposite sides of an altar. The intricate floral accents are placed among the spiraling candles, creating a colorful setting for your celebration. This beautiful array of flowers, including gladioli, snapdragons, stock, gerbera daisies, roses, miniature carnations and statice, enhances a peachtone color scheme. The coordinating altar arrangement echoes the spiral effect of the candles, providing the finishing touch to this enchanting display of flowers and candlelight.

One of the most popular ways to create a romantic mood at your evening wedding is with candlelight. Using flowers to decorate the candelabra that hold the candles is an elegant and stylish way to enhance your wedding ceremony. Candelabra come in a variety of shapes, sizes and colors, with the most common style being the seven-branch. This style holds seven candles and can be adjusted to several positions to create just the right look. Another popular type of candelabra is the spiral. This style holds fifteen candles and can be positioned so that its branches form an elegant spiral. There are many other styles and shapes available, including nine-branch, three-branch, heart-shaped and individual styles that attach to the end of a pew. The three-branch candelabra style is often used as a standing unity candle. Candelabra come in many finishes, including brass, white, gold and black, to help you create just the right look.

You can create simple or elaborate displays with candelabra, depending on the number and style you choose to use. A pair of matching candelabra, one positioned on each side of the altar, is the very least you will want to use. Most of these candelabra styles hold taper candles, which come in a variety of colors and lengths to complement your floral look. The many dripless candles available will not make a mess while they are burning, or you may choose mechanical candles, which also are dripless.

Once you have selected the style of candelabra you would like for your wedding, it is important to finish the look with a beautiful floral accent. You can choose something simple like a lovely bow or bow and foliage combination, or you can opt for a more elaborate display of flowers. The flowers you choose should complement the style of the wedding and coordinate with the other flowers you have selected.

Candelabra are usually rented from your florist or party rental service, or they may be available at the church. The price of a rental may not include the cost of the candles; the cost of the floral arrangement will be extra. Make sure that you clearly understand what is included in the quoted price.

As noted before, there may be restrictions on the use of open flames in the church or city where you are holding your wedding. Be sure to check on this before making arrangements to have candelabra at your wedding. Your professional floral consultant will be able to help you with all the details of renting candelabra for your wedding. If you are able to use candelabra, the glow of their candles can be a wonderful way to light the way to your bright future.

This seven-branch candelabra base is adjustable to form different shapes, including angled or pyramid shapes such as shown here. The candelabra features glowing 18" taper candles accented with flowers in vibrant jeweltone colors. The floral accent is designed to accentuate the form of the candelabra, and includes "Kiss Proof" lilies, purple larkspur, burgundy carnations, red roses, lavender stock and purple asters.

Romance is in the air with this white seven-branch candelabra accented with a delicate combination of pink and white flowers. Pink and white carnations, miniature carnations, white stock, bridal pink roses and lily blossoms fashion the floral accent while sheer pink fabric drapes to the floor, creating an enchanting, romantic look.

A glowing chapel setting is created by using standing candelabra and candles on the altar. Nine-branch candelabra are trimmed with lush foliage garlands made with sprengeri, salal, variegated pittosporum and strands of ivy. The classic look of mixed white flower arrangements adorns the base of the candelabra and the area above the altar. Candle displays also decorate the altar to complete the look.

A white nine-branch candelabra accented with a delicate floral garland is an attractive choice to decorate your wedding. Light pink gerbera daisies, miniature carnations, pompons, white spray roses and baby's breath form the garland. Streamers of pink and burgundy ribbon are intertwined with the flowers and left to trail below, completing the design.

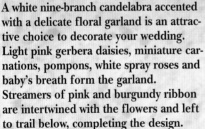

A three-branch candelabra with candles in glass hurricane globes is decorated with a striking mixture of star gazer lilies, purple dendrobium orchids, delphinium, red, orange and burgundy carnations, orange tulips, lavender liatris and bright pink miniature carnation blossoms. The splash of color is accented by a star gazer lily tied to the main floral design with vibrant orange ribbon. This candelabra display is perfect for a summer or fall wedding, and can also be used as a standing unity candle display. You might also select one of the three-branch candelabra styles that can be attached to a pew for your aisle decorations.

$\mathcal{P}ew$

DECORATIONS

A classic look is created by combining an elegant white satin ribbon bow with delicate sprengeri and plumosa foliage. This simple pew decoration can be used for all types of wedding ceremonies. The beautiful bow can be fashioned from any number of ribbon colors to create the look just right for you.

Fresh, vividly colored flowers adorn the pew with their natural beauty. This vibrant floral accent is made with yellow gerbera daisies, hot pink carnation blossoms, purple "Matsumoto" asters and yellow freesia. Placed on several pews, this lovely pew arrangement will create a beautiful pathway for the bridal party.

$\mathcal{B}$eautiful pew decorations create an enchanting path to follow as you make your entrance and walk down the aisle. Floral adornments on the ends of the pews or chairs will also make a striking impression on your guests as they are escorted to their seats. Pew decorations can be used to expand upon the look of the altar flowers by turning the space of the entire church into a romantic wedding setting.

The floral looks that you can create for decorating the end of a pew or chair are endless. From delicate combinations of mixed flowers to simple bows made of satin ribbon, your floral consultant will be able to help you create just the right look to coordinate with the style of the wedding. Pew decorations can be placed on every row, every other row or every third row, depending on the result you desire. They can also be used to designate seating areas for family and special guests. In some instances, pew decorations can be removed and used at reception locations. Your floral consultant will be able to help you determine whether this is possible.

A stylish wreath placed on the end of a classic wood pew reflects a personal touch. This natural wreath is formed with ivy and accented with champagne sweetheart roses, peach statice and pink sheer ribbon, creating a delicate alternative to traditional pew decorations.

Soft, delicate tulle accented with peach roses and baby's breath expresses love and innocence for the romantic bride. Pastel-colored roses combined with the enchanting look of airy tulle fabric will add a memorable look to your wedding flowers.

Floral
ACCESSORIES
FOR WEDDINGS

There are many ways to add the beauty of flowers to your wedding ceremony besides traditional altar arrangements, candelabra and pew decorations. Be creative! The possibilities are endless — you can adorn windowsills, doors of entryways, church gates, pedestals, and guest book tables. Any interesting characteristic of the setting of your ceremony can be enhanced with flowers.

A special part of many religious services is the kneeling bench. The kneeling bench can be decorated with fresh flowers that coordinate with the rest of your wedding flowers to create a distinctive look. Many churches have kneeling benches to use for wedding ceremonies; you can also rent one if the church or other location you are using does not offer one. Your floral consultant can offer suggestions on the rental and decoration of kneeling benches for your wedding.

Flowers enhance the overall look of your wedding ceremony, adding warmth and natural beauty. Be sure to work with your floral consultant to explore all the interesting possibilities available for floral decoration.

Church windows needn't be left plain when by placing an arrangement of flowers on a windowsill you can add decoration to the sides of the sanctuary or chapel. Here a simple hurricane candle arrangement adds another touch of candlelight to the ceremony. When selecting floral treatments for windows, be sure they enhance the church window and do not detract from its natural beauty.

Twin kneelers can be placed side by side, angled or facing each other, depending on the church and the area where they will be set. This setting features twin kneeling benches side by side accented with three flower arrangements. Orange lilies, peach roses and statice are combined with maidenhair fern to create these delicate arrangements. The accents are connected by satin ribbons draped between, completing a distinctive look easily recreated in many other colors.

Delicate flowers with a ribbon accent are placed on the side of this kneeler, creating a striking look. This floral accent, perfect for a peach color scheme, is designed with sonia roses, peach spray roses, pink carnations and miniature carnations, peach alstroemeria and statice. Sheer, iridescent ribbon spirals down from the flowers at the top to a smaller accent at the base of the kneeler to fashion an elegant look.

Create an enchanting entrance and greeting for your wedding guests with a beautiful door accent. This classic foliage wreath is accented with champagne sweetheart roses, white veronica, bouvardia and satin ribbon. The sight of a beautiful floral wreath on the church door will also let people know that a wedding is in progress.

53

Outdoor
WEDDINGS

A garden wedding on a beautiful summer day is a dream come true. The site can be enhanced with colorful mixtures of flowers that look as though you've just picked them from the garden. Large displays of brightly colored flowers create a stunning background, and provide an exciting accent to the lush green foliage. Scattered rose petals and potted chrysanthemums in several colors line the garden path that becomes the aisle. Romance is clearly in the air in this beautiful garden setting.

An elaborate garden flower arrangement featuring star gazer lilies, blue delphinium, white larkspur, and pink snapdragons can be used to grace any number of locations in your garden setting.

Your beautiful outdoor ceremony is not complete until you have decorated the gates, trellises, archways and other entrances into the romantic garden setting. This lovely gate accent uses star gazer lily blossoms, yellow alstroemeria, purple delphinium, Queen Anne's lace, purple statice and red miniature carnations to fashion an enticing look.

The natural beauty and splendor of gardens, parks and other outdoor locations can provide a wonderful setting for your wedding. Whether you select your parents' backyard or a beautiful rose garden, the setting can be enhanced with exquisite floral displays. The addition of fresh floral arrangements, potted blooming plants, foliage plants and even shrubs to a natural outdoor setting can create a romantic look.

If you have selected an outdoor site, be sure to visit the location with your floral consultant. Highlight all the points of interest that attracted you to this location. This will give your floral consultant a better understanding of your personality and what kind of setting you are interested in creating. It will also provide him or her with a chance to see the various natural elements that are available to work with.

When planning an outdoor wedding ceremony, it is a good idea to decide on a backup location in case of inclement weather. The floral designs you select can easily be transferred to this new location in case the weather changes your plans on the day of the wedding. Another idea is to set up a tent and decorate it with beautiful plants and flowers, which will let you enjoy your day undisturbed even if the weather does not cooperate. Tents can be rented from party rental companies.

An outdoor wedding can be a grand event if your setting is enhanced with flowers and plants that capture its essence. Your floral consultant can help you turn your garden wedding fantasy into an everlasting memory.

Crisp white chairs set in a natural garden create a striking complement. Decorate these chairs with a vibrant mixture of flowers that coordinate with the other flowers you have selected. Floral accents placed on the chairs will also accentuate the garden path you have created for the aisle.

A lovely garden wedding by the water will charm guests and make the day a memorable one. A white latticed canopy with matching screens and pedestals forms a gazebo-look background for this enchanting setting, complete with climbing vines. Beautiful arrangements styled in pink and lavender tones create a natural enhancement. The aisle is decorated with small floral accents attached to pedestals and chairs, with ribbon draped between to designate the garden path. Whether this canopy is used as a huppah in a Jewish ceremony or as an enhancement for a garden wedding, the setting will create lasting memories.

Create a tropical wedding setting in any outdoor location with this exciting mixture of fresh fruit and mixed flowers in festive display. An arch adorned with flowers marks the center of the site, with a kneeling bench and aisle carpet providing additional enhancement. Topiaries placed on either side of the aisle create a framing effect for the flower-accented arch. Large ferns and other green plants are placed in various locations to complete the look. Orange lilies, yellow daisies, yellow, tangerine and ivory carnations, purple asters and yellow roses are combined to create a unique and brightly colored wedding setting.

THE Jewish TRADITION

This romantic huppah setting is created by covering a decorative metal frame with yards of fluffy white tulle or illusion fabric. The delicate flowers and pure white satin ribbon accentuate the soft, cloudlike feeling created by the fabric. Dainty sprengeri foliage spills from each arrangement at the top of the canopy. A small floral arrangement accents the table, which is trimmed in braided ribbon.

Pastel-colored flower arrangements add to the beauty of the setting, while graceful foliage arrangements and plants surround the huppah to provide the finishing touch.

The huppah is the focus of this traditional setting for a Jewish wedding. This canopy made of sheer fabric, embroidered silk, satin, or other materials symbolizes both the nomadic tents or shelters of ancient Israel and the new home the bride and groom will share. When decorated and embellished with fresh flowers and foliage, it provides an absolutely gorgeous setting for the ceremony, rich in heritage and symbolism.

The huppah should form the center for the floral enhancements at the Jewish ceremony. Other floral arrangements can be placed in front, to the sides or on pedestals. Large urns or interesting pedestal looks featuring large arrangements help intensify the dramatic look of the canopy. Foliage plants can also enhance the look.

While the huppah has important religious significance in a Jewish wedding, an attractive canopy can be used to create a beautiful background or setting for a nonchurch ceremony of any faith.

This delicate mixture of pastel-colored flowers fashions a romantic illusion to coordinate with the huppah above. Tulle fabric entwined among the flowers creates the effect of a veil among the flowers, making this the perfect arrangement to complement and enhance this setting for a wedding ceremony.

Elegantly draped fabric and classic columns form the base of this beautiful huppah. Vibrantly colored mixed flower arrangements add to the wonder of the setting. Gerbera daisies, lilies, freesia, roses, carnations and delphinium are among the bounty of flowers used for the floral accents. Trails of sprengeri foliage and smilax garlands enhance the sweeping fabric background to create this wonderful look.

The arrangement placed on top of the high column in front is balanced with the large urn arrangement in the rear corner of the setting to create a stylish look. Elegant gold chairs trimmed in flowers form an exquisite aisle leading to the huppah. This dramatic look is appropriate for the most formal of ceremonies.

Reception Flowers

With the magic of your wedding ceremony still fresh in the hearts and minds of those attending, you can continue the wonder of the day by dazzling your guests with beautiful reception flowers. Whether you have selected the charm of your parents' backyard or the plush elegance of a five-star hotel, flowers will help you continue the theme of the ceremony by expressing your personal style.

In this section you will find many floral ideas that you can use to build the vision of your wedding reception. From elegant table settings to magnificent cake displays, these pages are filled with captivating images of beautiful wedding flowers. Combine these ideas with those of your professional floral consultant, and add the individual characteristics of the location of your reception to create a memorable look.

The overall look of your wedding reception can vary, depending on the style or theme you select. From elegant to whimsical, there are any number of settings you can create. Elegant, formal receptions are easily achieved if you select a location that fits this style, such as a stylish, older hotel or country club setting. Simple, carefree settings can be created in backyards, parks and contemporary hotels. Whatever setting you select for your reception, it should follow the themes you have established with your wedding ceremony.

There is an endless variety of floral ideas to enhance just about any setting for your wedding reception. Once you have selected the location and style that are right for you, work with your floral consultant to create the magical setting you've dreamed of.

A bountiful summer setting is created by combining yellow and teal accents with a colorful mixture of garden flowers. Beautiful ivy topiaries are accented with lush fruits and satin ribbon to add a fresh look to a buffet table adorned with a basket of flowers. Candleholders in a base of ivy coordinate with the look of the topiaries, and crisp yellow ribbons are tied into bows on the napkins. The result is an original look for a wedding reception.

Regal gold tones are featured in this exquisite setting. The metallic gold theme is carried throughout with gold floral containers, brass candlesticks, gold-wrapped chocolates, gold doilies and gold tassels adorning the napkins. Include small gifts trimmed in gold for your guests. These rich gold images are set against a background of elegant white.

Create an interesting look at your reception by introducing several different flower styles at the guest tables. A floral centerpiece on one table is complemented by small taper candles grouped under a hurricane globe and accented with a floral wreath on another. When placed in a large dining room, this variety provides an exciting look.

Whichever ideas you choose of the ones presented here, the look you create will be memorable.

An African violet plant in a small basket is decorated with ribbon trims. Miniature African violet plants are placed at each plate to enhance the look of the table setting and provide a small wedding remembrance that each guest can take home.

There are many ways to create just the right look at your wedding reception. One of the most important elements that will affect the final look of the event is the centerpiece you select. From fresh flowers to beautiful flowering plants, the possibilities are endless. With so many ideas to choose from, be sure to work closely with your floral consultant to choose the best floral idea to carry out the theme you have selected.

The centerpieces you select for the guest tables should contribute to the overall look you are trying to achieve. If you have chosen a large ballroom for your reception, you will want to decorate with elaborate raised floral centerpieces. If a smaller, more casual gathering is your style, the centerpieces should reflect this feeling. From casual to elegant, there is a centerpiece to fit every wedding style.

If you are planning a head table for the bridal party, choose floral decorations that coordinate with the arrangements you have selected for the guest tables. This will help you achieve an attractive, harmonious setting.

The look of the centerpieces you choose can be enhanced by the color and design of the table-cloth you select. The use of interesting textures, designs and colors in your table coverings can set the tone for the entire setting and greatly add to the overall look of your reception.

As with the church, if you plan to use candles in your table arrangements or in votive cups around the arrangements, be sure to check the local regulations at the location of your reception for any restrictions on the use of candles.

A trio of small glass vases filled with a variety of flowers creates an interesting centerpiece look. Use individually or all together to create just the right centerpiece for your wedding. Place a cluster of vases on one table or individual vases with different flowers on each table, add ribbon, or a fabric cluster at the base — whatever your fancy. This versatile idea can be used to create many different looks and fit any wedding color scheme.

A simple basket is brimming with flowers in this delicate centerpiece. Plumosa foliage and satin ribbon wrap the basket handle to create a dainty look, while roses, lilies, carnations, yarrow and larkspur provide the floral touch.

Delicate pink geranium blossoms are accented with a sheer fabric collar and a pastel basket. Perfect for a casual summer gathering or bridal shower, this centerpiece is sure to catch the eye of your guests.

The beauty of an outdoor wedding reception is captured in this lovely setting. Here the floral arrangement for a guest table is made in a white painted basket filled to the brim with an exquisite garden flower mix. A peach satin bow adorns the handle of the basket to coordinate with the tablecloth. Flower petals are sprinkled on the peach tablecloth, extending the effect of the centerpiece to the entire table.

This dainty arrangement featuring champagne sweetheart roses, daisy pompons, freesia and miniature carnations conveys the feeling of an afternoon tea. The delicate coloring of the tablecloth coordinates with the soft colors in the arrangement, creating a gentle pastel look suitable for a guest table at a wedding reception or a centerpiece at a bridal shower.

In addition to using centerpieces to enhance the guest tables at your wedding, you can use other enhancements on the plates and napkins to dress up the look. Here a small napkin ring that is part of a vase holds the napkin at the side of the plate. A small accent of freesia and rose blossoms fills the vase.

From summer to fall, this vibrant arrangement has great appeal. Cording accents the rich tones of the flowers to give the arrangement a regal look. Yellow roses, orange lilies, pink asters, red tulips, blue cornflowers and Chinese miniature carnations are combined and set against the background of a bright yellow tablecloth, creating a stunning effect.

ELABORATE *Floral* CENTERPIECES

Decorate your tables with elaborate centerpieces that rise from the table for a look that is sure to impress. Centerpieces styled with risers are an excellent way to fill the volume of space in large ballrooms and dining rooms, while at the same time allowing guests ample view of others seated at their table and the room itself.

An elaborate riser centerpiece features an arrangement at the base and an element that lifts a second arrangement high into the air. The two arrangements will usually match or be made of coordinated materials. Another way to achieve a similar look is with a topiary, an arrangement featuring a sphere formed of foliage or flowers suspended by a riser from a base container. Both types of arrangements form impressive floral displays when used on multiple tables in an open room space.

Imagine your reception filled with the beauty of these beautiful centerpieces. An elegant blend of white flowers including roses, lilies and miniature carnations forms the base arrangement, with dendrobium orchids added to the top arrangement to provide a trailing effect. Lush green ivy is also included to add movement to the entire arrangement. This classic setting is suitable for a wedding in any color scheme or if you prefer, you can add a splash of color to this striking display.

This colorful riser arrangement features a beautiful combination of flowers including gerbera daisies, lilies, roses, freesia, spray asters and pompons. Eucalyptus is added for enhanced fragrance, and caspia provides the lacy look. The arrangement is made in a container that is designed to hold candles in the top. The glowing effect of candlelight offers an added delight.

A topiary arrangement is formed with a lush green ivy and boxwood sphere suspended with natural twigs above a terra cotta pot. A simple bow on the pot provides added decoration. Notice how the centerpiece coordinates with the ivy-enhanced tablecloth. This natural but elegant arrangement is suitable for many different types of settings including an outdoor garden wedding.

Buffet

ARRANGEMENTS

*I*n addition to the flowers you choose for the head table and guest tables at your reception, you will want to add the beauty of flowers to dessert, hors d'oeuvre and buffet tables. Flowers enhance a food presentation in an elegant way and add to the overall feeling you are trying to create. Include candles, fabric and ribbon with your floral displays to fashion interesting and romantic looks. The use of pedestal containers and flower risers will lift the flowers off the table to make the food and flower displays even more impressive. Be creative about the use of flowers at your reception. Loose flowers tucked here and there as well as large floral arrangements all contribute to the splendor of the event.

A coffee and dessert table is accented with this beautiful vase of stock, roses, asters and bouvardia. The pastel look of the flowers is coordinated with ribbon tied to the vase and spilling onto the table. Used at a smaller home reception or tucked into a special corner of a larger dining room, this delicate vase looks as good as the sweet treats on the table.

Accent the corner of the dining room with an elaborate display of fruit, champagne and flowers. The glow of candlelight will entice your guests to taste the lush fruit and sample the bubbling champagne. The rich tones of the flowers accentuate the natural colorings of the fruit. Gold-trimmed ribbons are tied to the champagne glasses to add a festive look to the table.

Tempting food abounds on this beautifully decorated hors d'oeuvre table. Elevated floral arrangements provide an exquisite backdrop for the assortment of tasteful delights. Sheer peach fabric woven through the arrangement provides a softening look. Glowing candles placed on several levels add to this appealing display.

WEDDING Cake
FLOWERS

An elegant four-tier wedding cake is accented with fragrant gardenias and white roses. A beautiful floral accent is placed at the top, while single gardenias cascade down to the base. Flower clusters and foliage surround the base of the cake to complete the look. A candelabra is accented with a single gardenia and trailing smilax, and a lace table-cloth provides an elegant base for the entire setting.

Create a romantic setting for your reception by decorating your wedding cake and cake table with flowers. Floral cake tops, flowers at the base of the cake, arrangements on table candelabra and flowers on serving pieces are just a few of the ways to incorporate floral accents into the setting of your cake table. Coordinate flowers for your cake with the floral look you have selected, or choose an accent that enhances the look of the cake. Add a special table covering that will coordinate elements on the table. Whether you choose a selection of white flowers to match the cake or add a splash of floral color to coordinate with your color scheme, flowers add a delicate appeal to your cake table. Your floral consultant will be able to help you create a memorable wedding cake setting.

Add a fragrant, tropical look to your wedding cake setting with fresh lemons and limes. Classic gardenias and stephanotis are accented with the lemons and limes cut into various shapes. The fragrance is fresh and the look is unique.

A pastel yellow cake and punch bowl are accented with a delicate mixture of lavender roses, yellow alstroemeria and white daisy pompons. A cake top and floral clusters adorn the cake, while a ring of coordinating blossoms surrounds the punch bowl. Floating blossoms provide the finishing touch to this lovely setting.

Gilded accents of ribbon and foliage are featured on this beautiful fondant wedding cake. White roses form the top and continue to spill from layer to layer to the top of the table. Rose petals surround the base of the cake. The gilded look is repeated on the cake serving piece, decorative candles and glasses for the toast. This elegant look is suitable for the most formal of events.

Add a decorative look to your cake table with an interesting tablecloth look, complete with fabric bows. This multilayer cake is decorated with an accent of dark and light peach roses and bouvardia. Gypsophila softens the look. Floral accents at the top and center of the cake are enhanced by the beautiful blossoms that encircle the bottom of the cake. The silver table epergne is filled with coordinating flowers to complete this charming setting.

Four distinctive floral accents decorate this traditional wedding cake. Striking flowers sit at the top of the cake with a festive cluster placed at the middle. Delicate petals are placed on the base layer with another striking cluster fashioned at the base. Coordinating flowers enhance the groom's cake and spill out to the table, forming a decorative accent.

Christmas splendor is captured in this festive holiday cake setting. White roses, gerbera daisies, miniature carnations and variegated holly are clustered at the top and middle layers and the base of the cake. The intricate lace tablecloth provides the perfect background for this holiday wedding cake.

This delightful pastel cake table setting has the look of spring-time. Delicate floral blossoms are sprinkled on the cake and form a cluster at the top, with additional blossoms placed around the base. Coordinating ribbon is tied to the serving pieces and candlesticks and also decorates the cake. The glasses for the toast are accented with a simple flower cluster to match.

The bounty of a fall harvest is presented in this stunning cake table setting. Rich falltone flowers including roses, gerbera daisies and chrysanthemums cascade from layer to layer. Gold cording enhances the look, with the fruit of the harvest tucked among the flowers to make it even more memorable.

Decorative floral accents are placed on the hood and doors and in the rear of this classic limousine to create a stylish look on this most special of days. The mixed flowers include carnations, pompons, asters and miniature carnations. Delicate sprengeri enhances the look of the flowers and provides movement in the accents.

*Y*our wedding celebration would not be complete without special transportation. Horse-drawn carriages and elegant limousines are among the most popular ways for the bride and groom to move from the ceremony to the reception. Be creative — depending on the style of your wedding and personal taste, there are many other unique types of transportation you can use. From antique cars to a party bus, you can choose the method of transportation that is just right for you.

Once you have selected your favorite method of transportation, make sure you decorate it to coordinate with the look of your wedding flowers. This will personalize the car, carriage or whatever you select to your wedding theme. By decorating your transportation, you will have successfully coordinated the entire look of your wedding day from start to finish, making the day of your dreams come true and a wonderful start to a happy ever after.

This elegant horse-drawn carriage is accented with beautiful mixed flower accents, including several ribbon styles which are intermixed for an exquisite look. A ride in this wonderful carriage with your groom will add to the romance and magic of the day.

WEDDING

Planning

INFORMATION

Glance

Your wedding day is a memory you will cherish forever.

As you walk down the aisle, the months of planning and hard work you've just completed will make this moment everything you've dreamed it would be. Detailed planning and organization are the keys to a successful wedding day. Early planning gives you more flexibility in the choices you will have in planning the wedding of your dreams. Allowing yourself enough time to plan will make the experience exciting and memorable.

There are a number of bridal planners, workbooks, and even computer programs available to help you organize the details. Early in your planning, select a method of organizing that fits your personality and use it. Be sure to keep it up to date. Keeping everything in one spot will also ease the planning process.

Time management is another important part of planning. Set goals and task completion dates so that you can see the progress you are making. This will help you avoid overlooking important details of your wedding plan. Achieving these goals in an organized fashion will help you focus and relax so you can enjoy other prewedding events. Remember, you are planning for what is undoubtedly one of the most memorable events in your life, and you want to be able to enjoy the entire experience.

This section of *Romantic Wedding Flowers* contains helpful tools to assist you with planning, especially in the area of selecting your wedding flowers. The wedding plan at a glance gives you space to keep all the important details of your wedding close by. A wedding flower ordering checklist, information on what to do when, traditional etiquette about who pays for what and monthly planning space for notes and reminders — all are included to help make ordering your flowers as easy as possible.

Bride's Name:_____
Address:_____
Home Phone:_____
Work Phone:_____

Groom's Name:_____
Address: _____
Home Phone: _____
Work Phone: _____

Wedding Date: _____
Time:_____
Location:_____
Contact Name:_____
Phone:_____

Reception: _____
Time:_____
Location:_____
Contact Name:_____
Phone:_____

Officiant:_____
Address:_____
Phone:_____

Florist:_____
Address: _____
Phone: _____

Rehearsal Dinner Time:_____
Address:_____
Phone:_____

Wedding Consultant: _____
Address: _____
Phone: _____

Number of Attendants:_____
Names/Phone:
_____
_____
_____
_____
_____

Bridal Shop:_____
Address: _____
Phone:_____

Cake:_____
Address: _____
Phone:_____

Registered for Gifts at:
    Store:_____
    Phone:_____
    Store:_____
    Phone:_____
    Store:_____
    Phone:_____
    Store:_____
    Phone:_____
    Store:_____
    Phone:_____

Photographer:_____
Address: _____
Phone:_____

Video:_____
Address: _____
Phone _____

Music:_____
Address:_____
Phone:_____

Checklist

You have selected your florist, wedding style and color themes, your bridal party is in place and a budget is set. Now, it's time to decide on your floral plan. Below you will find a wedding flower ordering checklist to help you outline your floral needs. Use this space to make notes about the number of family and friends you will need flowers for, types of flowers you are interested in and would like to know more about, notes about the church and reception locations, etc. Capture as many thoughts as you can about your floral needs and use this as a guide when you meet with your florist. Providing your florist with these important details will enable him or her to get to know you better and help ensure that all your questions will be answered.

BRIDE
Color and Style of Gown_____
_____
Style of Bouquet_____
_____
Flowers_____
_____
Hairpiece_____
_____
Going Away Corsage (optional)
_____

JUNIOR BRIDESMAIDS
Number_____
Color and Style of Dress_____
_____
Style of Bouquet_____
Flowers_____
_____
Hairpiece Flowers_____

MOTHER OF GROOM
Color of Dress_____
Corsage_____
Purse Accent_____
Other_____
Flowers_____
_____

GROOM
Boutonniere Flowers_____

RING BEARER
Number_____
Boutonniere Flowers_____

GRANDFATHERS
Number_____
Boutonniere Flowers_____

HONOR ATTENDANTS
Number_____
Color and Style of Dress_____
_____
Style of Bouquet_____
_____
Flowers_____
_____
Hairpiece Flowers_____
_____

FLOWER GIRLS
Number_____
Color and Style of Dress_____
_____
Style of Bouquet_____
Flowers_____
_____
Hairpiece Flowers_____

GRANDMOTHERS
Number_____
Color of Dress(es)_____
Corsage Flowers_____
Other_____
_____
_____

BEST MAN
Boutonniere Flowers_____
_____

FATHER OF BRIDE
Boutonniere Flowers_____
_____

USHERS
Number_____
Boutonniere Flowers_____

BRIDESMAIDS
Number_____
Color and Style of Dress_____
_____
Style of Bouquet_____
_____
Flowers_____
_____
Hairpiece Flowers_____
_____

MOTHER OF BRIDE
Color of Dress_____
Corsage_____
_____
Purse Accent_____
Other_____
Flowers_____
_____

OTHER
_____
_____
_____
_____
_____

GROOMSMEN
Number_____
Boutonniere Flowers_____

FATHER OF GROOM
Boutonniere Flowers_____

OTHERS
Number_____
Boutonniere Flowers_____

VOCALIST
Number_____
Corsage Flowers_____
Boutonniere Flowers_____

READER
Number_____
Corsage Flowers_____
Boutonniere Flowers_____

GUEST BOOK ATTENDANT
Number_____
Corsage Flowers_____
Boutonniere Flowers_____

HOSTESS
Number_____
Corsage Flowers_____

HOST
Number_____
Boutonniere Flowers_____
_____

HONORED GUESTS
Number_____
Corsage Flowers_____
Boutonniere Flowers_____

Ceremony Flowers

ARRANGEMENTS FOR ALTAR
Number_____
Flowers_____
_____

OTHER ARRANGEMENTS
Number_____
Flowers_____
_____

UNITY CANDLE
Style_____
Flowers_____
_____

CANDELABRA
Number_____
Style_____
Flowers_____

AISLE/PEW DECORATIONS
Number_____
Style_____
Flowers_____

FOLIAGE PLANT RENTALS
Number_____
Style_____
_____
_____

CANOPY
Style_____
Flowers_____

KNEELING BENCH
Style_____
Flowers_____

AISLE CARPET
Length of Aisle_____
_____

OTHER
_____
_____
_____
_____

OTHER
_____
_____
_____
_____

OTHER
_____
_____
_____
_____

Reception Flowers

BRIDAL TABLE
Centerpiece Flowers_____
Other Flowers/Accents_____
_____
_____

GUEST TABLES
Number_____
Centerpiece Flowers_____
Other Flowers/Accents_____

CAKE TABLE
Cake Flowers_____
Other Flowers/Accents_____
_____

BUFFET TABLE
Number_____
Arrangement Flowers_____

GUEST BOOK TABLE
Flowers/Accents_____
_____

GIFT TABLE
Flowers/Accents_____
_____

BOUQUET TO THROW
Style_____
Flowers_____
_____

OTHER
_____
_____
_____

OTHER
_____
_____
_____

Rehearsal Dinner

CENTERPIECES
Number_____
Flowers_____
_____

OTHER
Number_____
Flowers/Accents_____
_____

BRIDE
Corsage Flowers_____

GROOM
Boutonniere Flowers_____

WEDDING AND BUDGET
Expenses

An organized, well-planned wedding always starts with the couple's determining a budget. The budget should include everything from your dress and flowers to the food, music and invitations. The style of wedding you choose along with the number of guests you are planning to invite will influence the budget you establish, as a more formal event will require a much larger budget than a simple wedding in the home.

Traditionally, the bride's family has been responsible for the majority of the wedding expenses, with the groom's family paying for specific, designated items. However, this is no longer necessarily true. Wedding expenses may be divided in whatever way the families wish, and are often split evenly. With the increased cost of weddings, today's bride and groom are sharing more of the expense with their parents, and they may even choose to pay for the entire wedding. It is best to discuss the subject with both families in order to work out the best solution for everyone.

The traditional division of wedding expenses is as follows:

An exquisite dress and striking bridal bouquet create an elegant look.

The Bride and/or Her Family

- Wedding invitations, announcements and mailing costs
- Engagement party (optional)
- Engagement and wedding photographs
- Entire cost of ceremony: location, music, rentals and all related expenses
- Transportation of wedding party to ceremony and reception
- Ceremony and reception flowers
- Gifts for bridesmaids
- Guest book for wedding

- Bride's wedding dress, veil and accessories
- The bride's personal trousseau and stationery
- Video
- Entire cost of reception: food, drink, entertainment, rental items, gratuities for bartenders and waiters, decorations and wedding cake
- Flowers for bridesmaids
- Groom's wedding ring and gift
- Hotel accommodations for out-of-town bridesmaids

The Groom and/or His Family

- Bride's engagement and wedding rings
- Clergy person's fee
- Groom's wedding attire
- Bride's wedding gift
- Gifts for ushers and groomsmen
- Accommodations for out-of-town ushers and groomsmen
- Rehearsal dinner

- Marriage license
- Flowers: Bride's bouquet and going-away corsage, boutonnieres for fathers and other men in the wedding party and corsages for mothers and grandmothers
- Complete honeymoon expenses
- Refreshments for reception (optional)
- Any other expenses they wish to assume

AND THE PLANNING
Begins

As we noted earlier, it is important to do your basic planning early. Follow this basic wedding "to do" list and you will be on your way to the magical day of your dreams.

An elegant pedestal arrangement created with beautiful pastel-colored lilies, gerbera daisies and roses.

Six to Twelve Months Before Your Wedding

- Choose a date and determine your budget.

- Decide on the style of wedding you would like to have: formal vs. informal; traditional vs. nontraditional; special themed event.

- Reserve locations for the ceremony and reception.

- Invite your clergy to officiate at your wedding.

- Select a photographer and a florist who will capture the essence of the wedding you have always dreamed about.

- Choose a caterer and a menu.

- Decide on entertainment for the reception and book musicians or disc jockeys, etc.

- Investigate other contract services you may need, including wedding cake specialists, video and rental companies (tuxedos, limousines).

- Announce your engagement in the newspaper.

- Determine your guest list. Make sure you consult your parents and the parents of your fiancé about the guests they would like you to invite, and ask them both to return a list by a specific date.

Next...

- Select your bridal party.

- Choose a color scheme to reflect your personality, complement your bridal party and enhance the decorations for the wedding celebration.

- Select your dress and hairpiece. It's important to note that some bridal dress manufacturers take up to six months to deliver special orders.

- Choose dresses for your bridal party. If they live far away, ask them for measurements and sizes.

Four Months Before Your Wedding...

- Order all wedding attire, including tuxedos or other attire for the groom and his party.

- Finalize the guest list.

- Order the invitations and announcements; start addressing the envelopes.

- Register at a bridal registry.

- Make final arrangements for contract services; pay deposits and sign contracts.

- Select your wedding rings.

- Order cake and finalize menu.

- Discuss color scheme with your mother and fiancé's mother so they can choose their gowns.

Three Months To Go...

- Arrange dress fittings for yourself and attendants.

- Make appointments for physical exams and blood tests (check state or local requirements).

- Decide on honeymoon destination and make reservations.

- Address invitations and announcements; they should be mailed 4 to 6 weeks before wedding.

Two Months Before Your Wedding...

- Finalize ceremony and review details with officiant.

- Schedule the wedding rehearsal and dinner.

- Shop for gifts for each other.

- Complete all official details such as marriage license or counseling (check local requirements).

- Handle financial and other legal details.

- Arrange beauty consultations (hairdresser, make-up, manicurist, etc.).

- Order any specialty items (such as imprinted napkins or matches).

Four to Six Weeks Before Your Wedding...

- Meet with service team members (photographer, florist, caterer, etc.) to finalize details.
- Schedule your formal portrait.
- Complete details of honeymoon.
- Send out your wedding invitations and announcements.
- Arrange final fittings for yourself and bridesmaids.
- Prepare wedding announcements for local newspaper.

Two Weeks Before Your Wedding...

- Coordinate plan for receiving gifts.
- Purchase gifts for bridal party.
- Contact guests who have not responded.
- Give caterer final count.
- Plan seating arrangement for reception.
- Confirm honeymoon plans.

One Week Before Your Wedding...

- Hold final meetings with contract services. Provide any final details, such as the list of pictures you want the photographer to take, any changes in music for ceremony or reception, delivery and set up times, etc.
- Review responsibilities of the bridal party.
- Pick up wedding rings and be sure they fit.
- Make sure everyone's wedding attire fits.
- During the last week. . . pick up your dress and any other final accessories.
- Pack for your honeymoon.

Multicolored ribbons are draped amongst flowers and candles, creating a lovely effect.

Bright yellow satin ribbon is the finishing touch to this clutch-style bouquet.

Your Wedding Day

- Relax, pamper yourself. Allow plenty of time to get ready. Forget about minor details — it's too late to change anything! Spend special moments with your family. Enjoy the day.

After Your Wedding...

- Send flowers or a thank-you gift to your parents.
- Send wedding announcements and pictures to the newspapers.
- Write and send thank-you notes for the gifts you received.

Ribbons spill from layer to layer, connecting the delicate floral accents that decorate this exquisite wedding cake.

A CHERISHED MEMORY YOU WILL HOLD FOREVER

Your Wedding Day

As you begin to make plans that will turn your wedding into a reality, be prepared to handle organizational demands and time management challenges. The following calendars will guide you through those busy months of preparation, excitement and anticipation. They will also provide a handy reference and gentle reminder of the important dates. The "notes" area can be used for any additional information you may want to keep at hand. Creative tips and ideas are also listed throughout to help make your wedding special.

 **Month of** _____

Notes: _____

_____

_____

SUNDAY	MONDAY	TUESDAY	WEDNESDAY	THURSDAY	FRIDAY	SATURDAY

 **Month of** _____

Notes: _____

_____

_____

SUNDAY	MONDAY	TUESDAY	WEDNESDAY	THURSDAY	FRIDAY	SATURDAY

 Month of

Notes: _____
_____
_____

SUNDAY	MONDAY	TUESDAY	WEDNESDAY	THURSDAY	FRIDAY	SATURDAY

Month of

Notes: _____
_____
_____

SUNDAY	MONDAY	TUESDAY	WEDNESDAY	THURSDAY	FRIDAY	SATURDAY

Month of

Notes: _____
_____
_____

Every aspect of love and romance is symbolized by the language of flowers. Select flower combinations to convey a special meaning.

SUNDAY	MONDAY	TUESDAY	WEDNESDAY	THURSDAY	FRIDAY	SATURDAY

Month of

Notes: _____
_____
_____

For wedding transportation and a unique departure, drive off in an antique convertible, horse-drawn carriage or trolley. Decorate with flowers for a festive touch.

SUNDAY	MONDAY	TUESDAY	WEDNESDAY	THURSDAY	FRIDAY	SATURDAY

 *Month of*

Notes: _____

_____

_____

SUNDAY	MONDAY	TUESDAY	WEDNESDAY	THURSDAY	FRIDAY	SATURDAY

Month of

Notes: _____

_____

_____

SUNDAY	MONDAY	TUESDAY	WEDNESDAY	THURSDAY	FRIDAY	SATURDAY

Month of

Notes: _____
_____
_____

On your wedding program, include an inspirational quotation, greeting, tribute or poem that you would like to share with your guests.

SUNDAY	MONDAY	TUESDAY	WEDNESDAY	THURSDAY	FRIDAY	SATURDAY

Month of

Notes: _____
_____
_____

Have guests throw bird seed, confetti or rose petals for good luck as you and your husband leave the ceremony or reception. For another creative alternative, have guests blow bubbles!

SUNDAY	MONDAY	TUESDAY	WEDNESDAY	THURSDAY	FRIDAY	SATURDAY

 Month of _____

Notes: _____
_____
_____

Intertwine tiny twinkle lights among flowers to brighten your reception and add an extra sparkle to the evening.

SUNDAY	MONDAY	TUESDAY	WEDNESDAY	THURSDAY	FRIDAY	SATURDAY

Month of _____

Notes: _____
_____
_____

Think about sending a small wedding photo to guests who couldn't attend. For those extra-special people, add a small floral bouquet created in some of the same flowers used at your wedding.

SUNDAY	MONDAY	TUESDAY	WEDNESDAY	THURSDAY	FRIDAY	SATURDAY

Index

Aisle Decorations 52
Alstroemeria 12
Altar Arrangements 48
Arm Bouquets 28-29
Arrangements 45-66
    Aisle 52
    Altar 48
    Buffet 62
    Cake 63-65
    Candelabra 50-51
    Canopy 56
    Car 66
    Carriage 66
    Centerpiece 59-61
    Huppah 56
    Kneeling Bench 53
    Outdoor 54-55
    Pew 52
    Unity Candle 49
Bouquet Styles 19-37
    Arm Bouquets 28-29
    Cascade Bouquets 20-21
    Clutch Bouquets 36-37
    Contemporary
      Freeform Bouquets 32-33
    Crescent Bouquets 24-25
    Rose Bouquets 26-27
    Round Bouquets 22-23
    Same Flower
      Bouquets 34-35
    Single Flower
      Bouquets 28-29
    Specialty Bouquets 30-31
Boutonnieres 42-44
Bouvardia 12
Bridal Bouquets 18, 19-31
    Carrying 18
    Selecting 18
Buffet Arrangements 62
Cakes 63-65
Candelabra 50-51
Canopy 56
Car 66
Carnation 12
Carnation, Miniature 12
Carriage 66
Cascade Bouquets 20-21
Centerpieces 59-61
Ceremony Flowers 45-56
Children, Flowers for 38-39

Chrysanthemum 12
Church Settings 46-47
Clutch Bouquets 36-37
Color .10
    Analogous 10
    Complementary 10
    Monochromatic 10
    Triadic 10
Colors, Popular Wedding 11
    Black 11
    Blue 11
    Green 11
    Peach 11
    Pink 11
    Purple 11
    Teal 11
    White/Ivory 11
    Yellow 11
Consultant, Wedding Flower 9
Contemporary Freeform
    Bouquets 32-33
Corsages 42-44
Crescent Bouquets 24-25
Floral Accessories, Ceremony . . .53
Floral Designer 9
Florist .9
Flower Availability 14-16
    Year-round 14
    Monthly 15-16
Flower Girl Flowers 38-39
Flowers, Popular Wedding 12-13
    Alstroemeria 12
    Bouvardia 12
    Carnation 12
    Carnation, Miniature 12
    Chrysanthemum 12
    Freesia 12
    Gardenia 12
    Gerbera Daisy 12
    Gypsophila 12
    Lily, Casablanca 12
    Lily, Star Gazer 13
    Orchid, Cattleya 13
    Orchid, Cymbidium 13
    Orchid, Dendrobium 13
    Orchid, Phalaenopsis 13
    Queen Anne's Lace 13
    Rose 13
    Rose, Sweetheart 13
    Stephanotis 13

Freesia 12
Gardenia 12, 35
Gerbera Daisy 12, 34
Gypsophila 12
Hair, Flowers for 40-41
Huppah 56
Lily .13
    Casablanca 13
    Star Gazer 13
Kneeling Bench 53
Monthly Planning Calendars . .74-79
Orchid 13
    Cattleya 13
    Cymbidium 13
    Dendrobium 13
    Japhet 13
    Phalaenopsis 13
Outdoor Weddings 54-55
Pew Decorations 52
Planning Timeline 72-73
Queen Anne's Lace 13
Reception Flowers 57-66
Reception Settings 58
Ring Bearer Flowers 38-39
Rose Bouquets 26-27
Rose 13, 26-27
    Sweetheart 13
Round Bouquets 22-23
Same Flower Bouquets 34-35
Single Flower Bouquets 28-29
Specialty Bouquets 30-31
Stephanotis 13
Unity Candle Arrangements 49
Wedding Budget 71
Wedding Cakes 63-65
Wedding Expenses 71
Wedding Flower Checklist 69-70
Wedding Flower Consultation 9
Wedding Flowers, Ordering 9
Wedding Plan at a Glance 68
Wedding Planning 67-79
    Budget 71
    Expenses 71
    Flower Checklist 69-70
    Monthly Planning 74-79
    Plan at a Glance 68
    Planning Timeline 72-73
Wedding Style 8
Wedding Themes 8
Wedding Transportation 66